HAL•LEONARD
INSTRUMENTAL PLAY-ALONG

AUDIO
ACCESS
INCLUDED

TROMBONE

QUEEN
UPDATED EDITION

PLAYBACK+
Speed • Pitch • Balance • Loop

To access audio visit:
www.halleonard.com/mylibrary

1809-4878-1498-1823

© Jorgen Angel/CTSIMAGES
Audio arrangements by Peter Deneff

ISBN 978-1-5400-3844-9

For all works contained herein:
Unauthorized copying, arranging, adapting, recording, Internet posting, public performance,
or other distribution of the music in this publication is an infringement of copyright.
Infringers are liable under the law.

Visit Hal Leonard Online at
www.halleonard.com

Contact Us:
Hal Leonard
7777 West Bluemound Road
Milwaukee, WI 53213
Email: info@halleonard.com

In Europe contact:
Hal Leonard Europe Limited
42 Wigmore Street
Marylebone, London, W1U 2RN
Email: info@halleonardeurope.com

In Australia contact:
Hal Leonard Australia Pty. Ltd.
4 Lentara Court
Cheltenham, Victoria, 3192 Australia
Email: info@halleonard.com.au

ANOTHER ONE BITES THE DUST

TROMBONE

Words and Music by
JOHN DEACON

Copyright © 1980 Queen Music Ltd.
All Rights Administered by Sony/ATV Music Publishing LLC, 424 Church Street, Suite 1200, Nashville, TN 37219
International Copyright Secured   All Rights Reserved

CRAZY LITTLE THING CALLED LOVE

TROMBONE

Words and Music by
FREDDIE MERCURY

Copyright © 1979 Queen Music Ltd.
All Rights Administered by Sony/ATV Music Publishing LLC, 424 Church Street, Suite 1200, Nashville, TN 37219
International Copyright Secured   All Rights Reserved

BICYCLE RACE

TROMBONE

Words and Music by
FREDDIE MERCURY

Copyright © 1978 Queen Music Ltd.
All Rights Administered by Sony/ATV Music Publishing LLC, 424 Church Street, Suite 1200, Nashville, TN 37219
International Copyright Secured   All Rights Reserved

BOHEMIAN RHAPSODY

TROMBONE

Words and Music by
FREDDIE MERCURY

Copyright © 1975 Queen Music Ltd.
Copyright Renewed
All Rights Administered by Sony/ATV Music Publishing LLC, 424 Church Street, Suite 1200, Nashville, TN 37219
International Copyright Secured   All Rights Reserved

FAT BOTTOMED GIRLS

TROMBONE

Words and Music by
BRIAN MAY

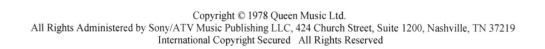

Copyright © 1978 Queen Music Ltd.
All Rights Administered by Sony/ATV Music Publishing LLC, 424 Church Street, Suite 1200, Nashville, TN 37219
International Copyright Secured   All Rights Reserved

I WANT IT ALL

TROMBONE

Words and Music by FREDDIE MERCURY,
BRIAN MAY, ROGER TAYLOR
and JOHN DEACON

Copyright © 1989 Queen Music Ltd.
All Rights Administered by Sony/ATV Music Publishing LLC, 424 Church Street, Suite 1200, Nashville, TN 37219
International Copyright Secured   All Rights Reserved

DON'T STOP ME NOW

TROMBONE

Words and Music by
FREDDIE MERCURY

Copyright © 1978 Queen Music Ltd.
All Rights Administered by Sony/ATV Music Publishing LLC, 424 Church Street, Suite 1200, Nashville, TN 37219
International Copyright Secured   All Rights Reserved

I WANT TO BREAK FREE

TROMBONE

Words and Music by
JOHN DEACON

Copyright © 1984 Queen Music Ltd.
All Rights Administered by Sony/ATV Music Publishing LLC, 424 Church Street, Suite 1200, Nashville, TN 37219
International Copyright Secured   All Rights Reserved

PLAY THE GAME

TROMBONE

Words and Music by
FREDDIE MERCURY

Copyright © 1980 Queen Music Ltd.
All Rights Administered by Sony/ATV Music Publishing LLC, 424 Church Street, Suite 1200, Nashville, TN 37219
International Copyright Secured   All Rights Reserved

KILLER QUEEN

TROMBONE

Words and Music by
FREDDIE MERCURY

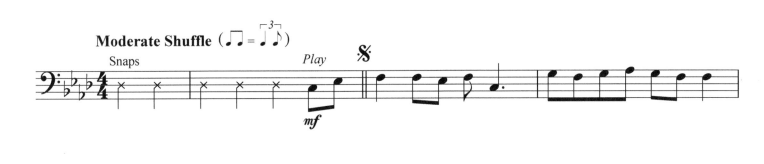

Copyright © 1974 Queen Music Ltd.
Copyright Renewed
All Rights Administered by Sony/ATV Music Publishing LLC, 424 Church Street, Suite 1200, Nashville, TN 37219
International Copyright Secured   All Rights Reserved

RADIO GA GA

TROMBONE

Words and Music by
ROGER TAYLOR

Copyright © 1983 Queen Music Ltd.
All Rights Administered by Sony/ATV Music Publishing LLC, 424 Church Street, Suite 1200, Nashville, TN 37219
International Copyright Secured All Rights Reserved

SAVE ME

TROMBONE

Words and Music by
BRIAN MAY

(small notes optional)

Copyright © 1980 Queen Music Ltd.
All Rights Administered by Sony/ATV Music Publishing LLC, 424 Church Street, Suite 1200, Nashville, TN 37219
International Copyright Secured   All Rights Reserved

SOMEBODY TO LOVE

TROMBONE

Words and Music by
FREDDIE MERCURY

Copyright © 1976 Queen Music Ltd.
Copyright Renewed
All Rights Administered by Sony/ATV Music Publishing LLC, 424 Church Street, Suite 1200, Nashville, TN 37219
International Copyright Secured   All Rights Reserved

UNDER PRESSURE

TROMBONE

Words and Music by FREDDIE MERCURY,
JOHN DEACON, BRIAN MAY,
ROGER TAYLOR and DAVID BOWIE

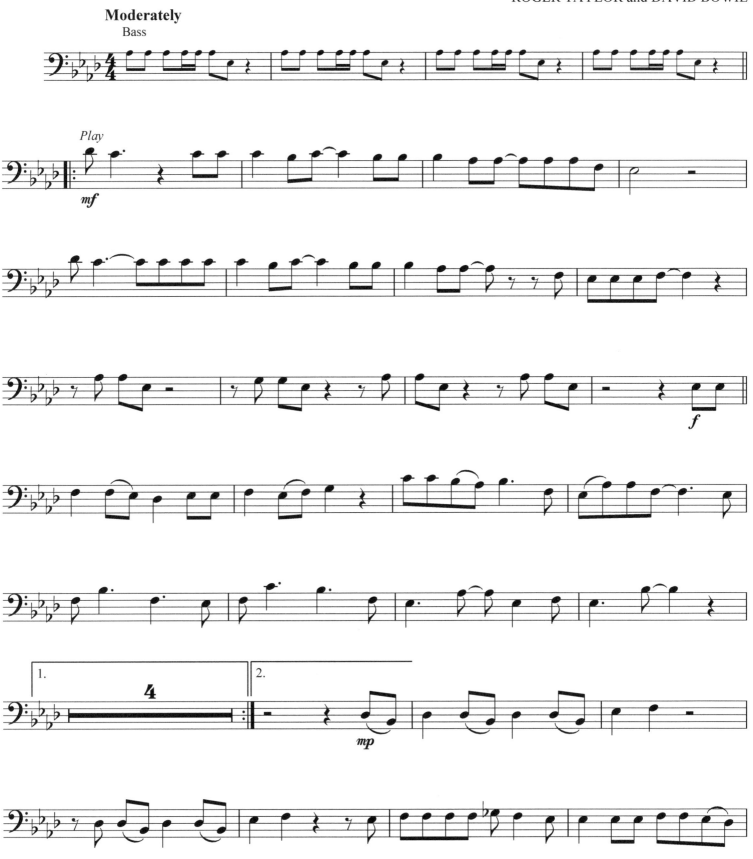

Copyright © 1981 EMI Music Publishing Ltd., Queen Music Ltd. and Tintoretto Music
All Rights on behalf of EMI Music Publishing Ltd. and Queen Music Ltd. Administered by
Sony/ATV Music Publishing LLC, 424 Church Street, Suite 1200, Nashville, TN 37219
All Rights on behalf of Tintoretto Music Administered by RZO Music
International Copyright Secured   All Rights Reserved

WE ARE THE CHAMPIONS

Words and Music by
FREDDIE MERCURY

TROMBONE

Copyright © 1977 Queen Music Ltd.
Copyright Renewed
All Rights Administered by Sony/ATV Music Publishing LLC, 424 Church Street, Suite 1200, Nashville, TN 37219
International Copyright Secured   All Rights Reserved

WE WILL ROCK YOU

TROMBONE

Words and Music by
BRIAN MAY

Copyright © 1977, 1978 Queen Music Ltd.
Copyright Renewed
All Rights Administered by Sony/ATV Music Publishing LLC, 424 Church Street, Suite 1200, Nashville, TN 37219
International Copyright Secured   All Rights Reserved

YOU'RE MY BEST FRIEND

TROMBONE

Words and Music by
JOHN DEACON

Copyright © 1975 Queen Music Ltd.
Copyright Renewed
All Rights Administered by Sony/ATV Music Publishing LLC, 424 Church Street, Suite 1200, Nashville, TN 37219
International Copyright Secured   All Rights Reserved